HAL•LEONARD
NSTRUMENTAL
PLAY-ALONG

AUDIO
ACCESS
INCLUDED

PLAYBACK+
peed • Pitch • Balance • Loop

CLARINET

TOP HITS

T0066169

Audio arrangements by Peter Deneff

To access audio visit:
www.halleonard.com/mylibrary

Enter Code
4803-9058-2678-0165

ISBN 978-1-4950-6573-6

HAL•LEONARD®
CORPORATION
7777 W. BLUEMOUND RD. P.O. BOX 13819 MILWAUKEE, WI 53213

Visit Hal Leonard Online at
www.halleonard.com

TITLE	ARTIST	PAGE
Adventure of a Lifetime	Coldplay	3
Budapest	George Ezra	4
Die a Happy Man	Thomas Rhett	6
Ex’s & Oh’s	Elle King	8
Fight Song	Rachel Platten	10
Hello	Adele	12
Let It Go	James Bay	14
Love Yourself	Justin Bieber	16
One Call Away	Charlie Puth	18
Pillowtalk	Zayn	20
Stitches	Shawn Mendes	22
Writing’s on the Wall	Sam Smith	24

ADVENTURE OF A LIFETIME

CLARINET

Words and Music by GUY BERRYMAN,
JON BUCKLAND, CHRIS MARTIN,
WILL CHAMPION, MIKKEL ERIKSEN
and TOR HERMANSEN

BUDAPEST

CLARINET

Words and Music by GEORGE BARNETT
and JOEL POTT

To Coda
D.S. al Coda
(no repeat)
CODA
mf

DIE A HAPPY MAN

CLARINET

Words and Music by THOMAS RHETT,
JOE SPARGUR and SEAN DOUGLAS

To Coda
7
D.S. al Coda
CODA
mf
mp
rit.

EX'S & OH'S

CLARINET

Words and Music by TANNER SCHNEIDER
and DAVE BASSETT

To Coda
3
D.S. al Coda
CODA
3
7
mf
f
1.
2.
3

FIGHT SONG

CLARINET

Words and Music by RACHEL PLATTEN
and DAVE BASSETT

1.
2.
D.S. al Coda
CODA
mp
2
mf
f
mp rit.

HELLO

CLARINET

Words and Music by ADELE ADKINS
and GREG KURSTIN

f
To Coda
D.S. al Coda
mp
CODA
1.
2.

LET IT GO

CLARINET

Words and Music by JAMES BAY
and PAUL BARRY

2.
To Coda
7
D.S. al Coda
CODA
7
mf
1.
2.
mp
1.
f
2.
8

LOVE YOURSELF

CLARINET

Words and Music by JUSTIN BIEBER,
BENJAMIN LEVIN and ED SHEERAN

ONE CALL AWAY

CLARINET

Words and Music by CHARLIE PUTH,
BREYAN ISAAC, MATT PRIME,
JUSTIN FRANKS, BLAKE ANTHONY CARTER
and MAUREEN McDONALD

f
mp
1.
f
2.
mf
rit.

PILLOWTALK

CLARINET

Words and Music by LEVI LENNOX,
ANTHONY HANNIDES, MICHAEL HANNIDES,
ZAYN MALIK and JOE GARRETT

To Coda
D.S. al Coda
(take 3rd ending)
CODA

STITCHES

CLARINET

Words and Music by TEDDY GEIGER,
DANNY PARKER and DANIEL KYRIAKIDES

To Coda
D.S. al Coda
CODA
4
1.
2.

WRITING'S ON THE WALL

from the film SPECTRE

CLARINET

Words and Music by SAM SMITH
and JAMES NAPIER